I AM NOT
BROKEN

I AM NOT BROKEN

Jo M

authorHOUSE®

AuthorHouse™
1663 Liberty Drive
Bloomington, IN 47403
www.authorhouse.com
Phone: 1 (800) 839-8640

Published by AuthorHouse   06/09/2015

ISBN: 978-1-5049-1581-6 (sc)
ISBN: 978-1-5049-1580-9 (e)

Library of Congress Control Number: 2015908914

Print information available on the last page.

Any people depicted in stock imagery provided by Thinkstock are models, and such images are being used for illustrative purposes only.
Certain stock imagery © Thinkstock.

This book is printed on acid-free paper.

Because of the dynamic nature of the Internet, any web addresses or links contained in this book may have changed since publication and may no longer be valid. The views expressed in this work are solely those of the author and do not necessarily reflect the views of the publisher, and the publisher hereby disclaims any responsibility for them.

For my family—all of them—for their love, support, and prayers. They have been beside me through it all and remain there today. I could not be who I am without them.

To the many doctors, nurses, aides, and therapists who cared for me: thank you for never making me feel as though it was time to give up.

A special thank-you goes to my son and daughter who have been put through situations that I would have never asked them to experience, and who faced those situations without hesitation. I would never have chosen to put either of you through the pressures and turmoil, but you both came through it shining brightly, and I am so proud of you both.

My beloved companion, my dog, Sandy Lou, has been calm, loving, funny, and understanding and the best company I could have ever asked for. We get well and stay well for one another.

> *To appeal to sympathy for pity's sake is to seek affirmation of the choice to do nothing.*

> — *Unknown*

Foreword

It is said that what doesn't kill you makes you stronger. To this I would usually add "and makes you more neurotic." Looking back, I have definitely lived, and I blame no one but myself for my troubles. I thank the good Lord for all of my recoveries. My hope is that my story will remind you and make you think about what is really important and what cannot be replaced. I wish to inspire you as he has inspired me. If I were asked to sum up my life in one sentence, it would be "He touched me."

I would rather laugh than cry because crying messes up your makeup.

—Author

Introduction

Some people are born with a silver spoon in their mouths, some with nothing more than love and hope ... and then there is me. I was born with a mouthful of sarcasm and humor. I have always used this to cover my pain and insecurities. It is what I do. I make no excuses for this, because it is what I am. I am also a survivor. I was married at seventeen years of age and had two children by the time I was twenty-one. I tried hard to be a good mother, a good wife, and a good employee. I realize now that it is not possible to be all three all the time, at least not in the way I thought I should. William had been married once before, and I really had no formal training or experience. All I had was a bunch of ideas, but after all, I was just a child myself. William started cheating on me after ten years had passed in our marriage. I waited for twenty years before I had an affair. I have since figured out that two wrongs do not make a right, and that is in no way the way the Lord meant for us to live.

I was told that I had an incurable disease and was dying, and then, right on time, I had a brain aneurysm and a stroke. I was forced to face a divorce and two devastating illnesses along with all of the complications. I went from living in a house to an upstairs to a small bedroom and then to hospital rooms. I made it back to the living, but to get there, I had to learn how to laugh, cry, walk, and write, but most of all, fight. This is my story.

Chapter One

WHO I AM

*It's never a question of resources, it is always
a question of resourcefulness.*

—Chris Howard

To understand who I am and how I got to where I am now is the smartest place to start. I have learned that a person's point of view is always from his or her own perspective, and that is where the ultimate decisions are made. I was always a smart student in school. I loved to read and to learn. I was, in essence, a nerd or geek or whatever term you are familiar with. To add to that, I was not the slim, tan, cool girl who was so popular at the time. So, needless to say, I was self-conscience and shy. I was one of four children in a very broken marriage. My parents finally divorced when I was fifteen years old. When my little world began to fall apart, I decided that, if I didn't have a "whole family," then I would simply have to make one of my own. By that time, my grandparents had retired to a small country town just outside of where I lived, and I loved being there. People were not so judgmental; they were nice, and they smiled and spoke to one another. The best part of all was that they seemed to like me. I felt at home in this small town, and I stayed there as much as I possibly could. I decided then that I wanted to live there, so I set out to fulfill my dream. It has been said that I am strong, but I prefer hardheaded, stubborn, dumb, lucky, and most of all, I am my own worst personal critic. I am naturally a slow learner and easily forget the painful lessons that I have been made to learn. I want to think that everyone deserves a second chance (or more). I am not sure yet about the final decision, so you be the judge.

I met William when I was sixteen years old, and I married him when I was seventeen. To keep the record clear, I was pregnant at the time, and my mother gave her permission and was also at the courthouse when we exchanged our vows. I loved everything about him. He was older by eight years and had been married once before, but he said he was ready to start a family and that he loved me. The first ten years were great, and all of my dreams seemed to have come true. We had two beautiful children, and though we were "poor," we were happy.

Things seemed to start changing shortly after my grandmother passed away. I was a health clinic manager working for a small country employer. I felt as though I mattered. I made a difference in people's life's every day. I was busy—overwhelmed at times—but still I thought I was having fun. In addition to my "importance," I had a great guy who made me smile, made me laugh, but most of all, I felt completely comfortable when I was with him. The down side to this was that he was someone else's husband. Mine had left me emotionally years before that ... around twenty or so years, to be exact. I remember back to one day when I was sitting at the kitchen table, going through recipes, crying because I had found "her" picture in my husband's wallet. I had never been one to snoop or cross the lines of privacy before, but his actions, his words, and his mannerisms had changed. His mood had so distinctly changed that

I knew something was terribly wrong. And there it was, inscription and all, with a heart by her signature. I kept the picture, and I did not tell him. I tried to pretend that everything was okay and that nothing had happened. He finally asked me if I had taken something out of his wallet that belonged to him. I began to cry and told him yes. He insisted that she was just a friend and a "nice Catholic girl." I saw right through his lie, and he knew it. We just kept going, as if everything was okay, but a strain on our relationship had begun to take a hold. My dream of happily ever after was shattered. My belief about true love was crushed, and my heart was broken. I found myself not wanting to watch certain television shows or movies; any love story was just a lie and not worth wasting my time on. The romance was gone. The kids were both young, around six and eight years old at the time, so I was devastated by the thought of divorce and being a single parent. The rock in my world had always been my Mammaw. She was a great woman to all who knew her. She and Pappaw were devoted Catholics who went to church regularly and encouraged all of us to do the same. I had gone to church with them often while I was growing up, and I had seen how their faith and belief system made them both happy and strong. Little did I know back then that it would be the same faith that would be with me for a long, long time.

My self-worth is not my net worth.

—Unknown

So when my world crumbled, I went to my Mammaw for advice. I expected a hug and her total support, but instead I got a lecture on marriage and holy matrimony. She said that, if being married was easy, then everyone would do it and be successful at it. She said that you don't run just because it gets a little hard. She said when you take your vows before God, you are promising to love your mate in the good times and the bad times. Then she said that it takes two people to create a problem and the same two to fix it. "And what about the children?" she asked. "They need their father in their lives, and he needs them." Her reaction took me aback. I was floored. This was not what I had been expecting. Where was the loving, supportive response that I so desperately needed? It took me years before I really understood why she had said what she did. I loved and respected her so deeply that I took all of the blame for my situation and headed home. My chin, head, and heart were hanging low. After that, things would be good for a while, and then something would change, and he would seemingly detached from me and the kids. He would anger easily, go off with his friends to drink, and shut down emotionally. He would basically shut himself out from the entire family. Each time, my heart knew where he was going and what he was doing. I tried so hard to be a good wife, a good mother, and a good Catholic. I worked hard at my job, I drove all the neighborhood kids to school, and even did the Little League thing. I volunteered for school functions when I could. I did all of this, thinking it would make a difference. I was silently ashamed when I showed up at a Little League function without a husband. It was the same way with family and other social gatherings. I was married, but single. I did not fit into any group. I was alone, and I was lonely, and I assumed it was all my fault. Years passed, and jobs changed for me, each time with better pay but more responsibilities. The kids grew, and family vacations stopped. He actually struggled to keep the kids interested in family vacations. We would let each one invite a friend so they would still have fun, just to keep the tradition alive. That worked, but only for a little while. It became painfully obvious that once the children were grown, there would be no more common ground for our marriage. One of the final stabs was when he paid my good friend, my older sister, and one of my neighbors to take me out on the town on our anniversary.

My potential is limitless.

—Natalie Ledwell

He actually gave them his credit card so they would have no reason to say no. I can't remember now if I was more hurt or more embarrassed by the whole event. I still went for whatever reason and tried to pretend everything was okay. I was really perfecting my acting, and I almost started believing myself at times. I would cry to my closest friends and had several "outsiders" tell me what a fool I was and how one-sided and unhealthy our relationship was. I started thinking more about a divorce. The biggest hurdle I faced was my Mammaw and her beliefs. I could not do anything to hurt or disappoint her. One of my old bosses, who was also a friend, said she was my conscience. He was more right than even I knew at the time. Then the unthinkable happened. Mammaw became seriously ill. I was scared at the thought of losing her. She had always been my rock, my stability, my grounding force, and my inspiration. Looking back, I believe the entire family felt that same way. My mother, her two sisters, and all of the grandchildren surrounded her with our love and support. Some of us—the ones who could—would take turns sitting with her while she was hospitalized. The doctors said that it was pneumonia and she would recover. She just had to; we all needed her so much. But she did not recover. She had a series of strokes and became unable to speak and communicate. She was awake and still with us, but unaware. I would drive to the hospital after work, and I took some time off when I was allowed to. Mammaw was eventually moved to a hospice facility. I did not go there, because I could not *bear* to acknowledge the fact that she was dying. I got a call at work from one of my cousins who told me that she was gone. My knees felt weak and began to shake, and my heart felt as though it had physically broken. I barely remember leaving that day or where I went. Life without Mammaw was numb. Just her hug could cure any hurt anyone had. I am proud to say that, from the time I was a small girl until the days that Pappaw and Mammaw died, every encounter with them began and ended with a hug and an "I love you." I knew without a doubt that they both loved me unconditionally, and I loved them in the same way. To this day, I cannot visit their graves without crying. I can't help myself. As odd as it may seem, even though Pappaw died first and my heart was broken, I knew that I still had Mammaw to guide me and heal my hurts so I could survive. After Mammaw's death, I felt very alone. I could only imagine that it was the same alone that orphans must feel when they learn the truth. I know that I had my two children, my husband, biological parents, and other family members, but still I felt stranded and abandoned. How could a God so full of love for me do this? Her death was not fair to me, or to the rest of the family. I wanted nothing more to do with religion or church. I started doing things that I had shied away from in the past. I even went skydiving! My friends started changing as well. Many of them had lovers and were spending time and money on themselves. They were, in my opinion then, what I needed to be like. Life for me began to change—whether it was for better or for worse was yet to be established.

I often sat and thought about all of the occasions on which I had done wrong in my marriage. I would fix chicken when I was angry just because I knew it was something my husband did not like. Many times I would fix greasy foods or something I was sure would upset his stomach when he had been out drinking. He would eat whatever I had prepared, and every time he would get an upset stomach without fail. What could he complain about? That I had cooked? I thought it was pretty darn brilliant at the time. I did not think once about how he might have felt or ask him why he had done the things he'd done. Did I say that I easily forgot? There was a message from God I was missing, and this was just the beginning of what was to come.

Ability is what you are capable of doing. Motivation determines what you do. Attitude determines how well you do it.

—Lou Holtz

Chapter Two

GOING DOWN

As this metamorphosis occurred, I met "him." He was handsome, kind, and very much a gentleman. He came in as a patient to the medical practice where I was working as the office manager. He would smile and look me in the eye each time he spoke as if he actually respected me. I was instantly infatuated with him. He began calling during the workday just to say hello and to see how my day was going. It was refreshing to have a man speak to me and be so kind, inquisitive, and interested in me. He said that I intrigued him. Suddenly I did not feel so ugly and undesirable, and it was wonderful. I began to feel like a real woman again. We began seeing each other as often as we could. I was (and still am) thinking he must feel the same way that I did about our relationship. My expectations were minimal in the beginning. I figured we would play for a little while and then he would be on his way. I was okay with that, because we were both married and nothing more could be felt. Somehow, weeks turned into months, then to years. We became friends and offered each other support along with the physical enjoyment that we shared. I never felt guilt for what I was doing, and over time I began to think I was falling in love with him. I never said those three words, and neither did he. I tried hard to keep things in the right perspective. My morals had definitely begun to falter. Our relationship went on for about four years, and then once again, life offered another change, this time in my career. I went from office manager of a small private medical practice to director of a rural health group. I was commuting forty-five minutes one way just to get there, but the pay and the opportunity were worth it. I felt the pay scale was good enough to start thinking about financial independence and divorce. I thought that I was happy. My husband had busied himself then with a small herd of cows, multiple pastures, and a collection of tractors, trailers, and farm equipment. He literally took a part of each day to go and check on the herd. He spent his weekends shredding pasture, moving hay, and watching his cows. I complained once, and he said that the cows were living, breathing creatures that needed constant care. He said it in a way that made me think I was not as important to him as his precious cows were. But that was okay, because I had my own place of comfort, and soon I would be filing for a divorce. Each time he would say or do something that hurt me, I would think to myself, *Go ahead, give me another reason.* I would take quiet joy in knowing I had my friend to lean on and hold. With life going on like it was, my energy levels began to lower. I was losing weight and felt physically exhausted. I also began to have a burning pain in my legs, arms, and chest. My arms and legs actually felt as though they had concrete covers on them weighing them down. I could hardly walk or lift anything. My mind began to feel as heavy and slow as my body was beginning to feel. I was not prepared for what happened next. I went to multiple doctors and specialists seeking a diagnosis to explain what was happening to me. I had far too many X-rays and tests to mention. Then I was sent to a rheumatologist. On the very first visit, he looked over my medical background, asked some questions, and examined me. He then said with the utmost of confidence that he knew what was happening to me and why, but most importantly, that I was not crazy. I began to cry—sob, actually—because three doctors I'd seen before him had said that it was all related to anxiety and stress. They had suggested I just take a pill to relax. They knew that, at the time, my son was in the army and was set to go to Iraq, my job was stressful, and my husband was basically uninvolved with my well-being. The doctors were partially right; I was just too stubborn to admit it. I felt as if I had finally found the right doctor. He ordered a series of blood tests to confirm his diagnosis and then wrote two words on a piece of paper. He handed me the paper and told me to research both of them, gather any questions that I might have, and return in a week for the official diagnosis and treatment plan. The two words he had written were *lupus* and *myositis*. He felt that knowledge and complete participation in the treatment plan was a patient's best chance. In fact, he required this level of commitment. It took only one blood test—*one test*—to confirm his thoughts, and that test was for a muscle enzyme called creatine kinase, or CPK. My result measured more than 800, which meant that I had a form of myositis (inflammation of the muscles). It is a rare muscle disease called polymyositis. My body was attacking my muscle groups, making them weak. The burning pain was from the muscle deterioration, which exposed the nerves. This is a disease with no known cause and no known cure. It is thought that it might be genetic, but being so rare, more research was (and still is) needed. The disease is also said to be progressive. The rheumatologist had been right from day one. I thought this man was a genius—and I still do—but he had a cold, hard side to his persona that I would soon discover.

The following week I returned to his office, alone and scared. I had told William of the importance of this visit, but he said he was too busy and had to work. I sat in the doctor's office in shock as he explained what modern medicine did know about this disease and how he had planned to treat it. He had three rules that I must comply with: Rule #1: No more high heeled shoes, only comfortable flats. "Fashion is no longer an option." In fact, all of the dress shoes that I had were hurting my legs and doing damage to my already-weakening muscles. Rule #2: I must be my own best advocate—stay informed and involved in the care plan. Rule #3: I must rest before I got tired. It was time to slow down and begin the long, slow fight for my independence, and ultimately, my life. I don't know of any words that I can use to describe what I felt at that moment. Suddenly, I was not the person I thought I was anymore. Everything changed instantly—*everything*! Self-image, self-worth, spirituality, sexuality—they had all been torn apart by the diagnosis. I would have to rebuild these beliefs from the ground up. At the time, I wasn't sure how to do this, or even why I should have to. All seemed pretty much lost, and I had no fight left inside of me. I wanted my Mammaw; I needed her desperately. I went into a state of depression. I would look at myself in the mirror and not recognize the woman who looked back. I had always related who I was to what I did for a living and how well I excelled at it. I could no longer work, and I could barely drive and care for myself. I felt as though I was nothing but a burden. The relationship issues between my husband and me were not helping matters. He seemed to want nothing to do with me, and he stayed away as much as he could. I couldn't imagine how any man could see me as a sensual woman if I were crippled. Just the thought of that made me feel sick. Why would my friend want to hang around now? I was sure God was punishing me. I thought he had crippled my legs so I could no longer raise them in adultery. I believed this with all of my heart. I thought I was being punished for being in a loving, caring relationship. I called this disease "my attitude adjustment from the big guy." He had made me lie down, so I would look up. That is what my Mammaw would have said if she were still alive. I kept remembering something else, though, that she had said often: "God will not give you a burden heavier than you can carry." With that belief and her faith and love inside me, I began to fight back.

If you must fall, then fall forward.

—Unknown

I love my rheumatologist, I really do, but he has a way about him that leaves me with mixed emotions. I often hated him and cried on the way to the elevator after an appointment in the beginning. Looking back, I was trying to cope with the diagnosis and not doing well at it. The doctor would ask me at each visit if I still felt like a victim. I was in constant pain, easily fatigued, and I was depressed. Yes, I felt like a victim—so what? He often mentioned my lack of spousal involvement and made remarks about my now "slightly chubby physique." He would refer to the disease as a boxing partner. He said it was not something you could train for and then crawl back into the ring and beat. "You cannot win against this disease" was his belief, and that is what he would tell me. Then he would tell me to not lose hope, because the disease could possibly be contained. Just when I would think that I could not possibly go back to his office, he would say something kind and remind me that I had enough fight and willpower inside me to continue. Did I say earlier that I forgot easily? I guess it was his "tough love" program. No matter what he said or how angry I got, his treatment plan was working. Initially he said that most patients are bound to a wheelchair within six months of diagnosis and spend long periods of time in hospitals or rehabilitation facilities from the complications of the disease and treatment. I took immunosuppressant's (chemotherapy in pill form) and steroids, and at one point, I was taking twenty-nine pills a day. I managed to stay away from the hospitals and rehabilitation facilities, and I refused to sit in a wheelchair and give up. This is where my stubbornness was an asset. I had even found an online support group to chat with. With everything going on, I still felt as if I was destined to die. I felt unable to help myself. The chemotherapy went on for twenty-one months, and I had to take steroids intermittently for pain control before my body decided it had enough. I was on the verge of kidney failure and was going to the lab every three days. I could still walk on my own with arm crutches, although I was slow and unstable. I could even drive. I went short distances, using cruise control instead of my legs to control my speed, but that completely exhausted me. Mostly, I just stayed at home in my own new version of prison.

Life can be challenging, but it can be rewarding.

—Unknown

My friend was great during all of this. He would call me almost daily to see how I was feeling and to see what the doctor may have said. He told me he would be there for me as much as he could, given the situation. When I cried, worried about the chemotherapy and losing my hair, he would comfort me. He said he had never been with a bald woman but thought he would want to if I lost all of my hair. He said we could get different colored wigs for me, and it would be like he was in bed with a different woman each visit. He told me that my hair did not matter to him. All my husband would say was that I looked bad. My friend was the reason I was able to go on each day. He had become my new rock of strength. We would still occasionally meet, when I had the energy, just to spend time together. It was during those times with him that I completely forgot about the pain and fatigue. It was great to get those breaks. He often told me I was a beautiful woman with a beautiful body, no matter what. He is solely responsible for showing me that I was still a woman, sexually intact. I will always be eternally grateful for that lesson and for him helping me to see it. I was still struggling with spirituality when my daughter bought me a book by Sylvia Browne called *Past Lives, Future Healings*. She had even marked paragraphs in the book for me to pay special attention to. This was the beginning to a whole new outlook on life. I know in my heart that my friend and this book are what saved me from my own hell. During all of this, William had acquired several trailers and hired a driver for his truck. I had taught him how to use the computer, and things seemed to be going well. I had adjusted to being at home and was becoming more aware of my thoughts and actions. My daughter gave birth to her first child, and my son was doing okay. This was what my friend called "another chapter in my life." Fast forward to Christmas Eve. I went to my family gathering alone as usual. William had said he was going to get his paperwork from the driver and then he would be there. I learned later that evening that he was checking "her" in to a rehabilitation facility for drug use. I realized that, every time he was supposedly "getting his paperwork," he was seeing her. On Sundays he would tell me he was going to do this, but I knew it was visitation day, and he was going to be with her. I felt insulted and hurt that he could be so committed to another person. I started being more observant, and I did not like what I was finding. I had found that he was spending money from his business account on her. Once I got in his truck to move it out of the driveway and found he had her belongings tucked in the backseat; he was planning to take them to her. In the pile, there was a fairly large stuffed animal. I took it out of the truck, dragged it in the dirt, and gave it to my dog to play with. Needless to say, William was quite angry with me and tried to tell me that it was for me. We both knew that it was not for me, and I felt relieved somehow knowing my dog had destroyed the gift. The fighting and tension had reached their peak again, and this time he moved out. I was happy and sad at the same time. I was really trying to be a better person, a better mother, a better wife, and a better friend—so why was this happening to me? During the first week after he moved out, I was full of mixed emotions. I was relieved there were no more tension and no more arguing in the house. I would not have to hear his phone ring, know it was her, hear the tone of his voice change, and watch him run outside so I could not listen to the conversation. I no longer had to listen to the television turned up way too loud for sixteen to eighteen hours a day at a volume I was sure that the neighbors could hear. There were no more rude comments or food crumbs on the counter. No more spilled drinks everywhere, and no more feeding my dog things she shouldn't have just to make me angry. He was not there to kick her just to upset me. He could certainly be an inconsiderate jerk. That part of him I was not going to miss. Silence and solitude set in, and I felt at peace. After we had divided the food from the pantry, I decided to go to the grocery store and restock it with the things I wanted. I also start cleaning the house and rearranging the furniture that was left to remove obvious empty spaces that showed that something was missing. The most obvious piece of furniture was his recliner. I called it "his throne" and often said I would like to put it on the driveway and set it on fire. I hated that chair and was glad to see it gone. At first my goal had been to clean up the dust bunnies where the furniture had been, but I was struck with a deeper sense to really clean my space of all of his negative energy. I cleaned for two days almost nonstop and then burned sage so that the smoke would purify the house, just to be sure. It felt good. I had made a small list of things I wanted from the grocery store that I would cook and enjoy, so I headed off. As I walked in to my favorite grocery store, I was overwhelmed with a single thought—I was, for the first time in my life, shopping for just one. It was an uneasy feeling, and a sense of loneliness began to take over. I stuck to my list and left without much conversation, and I cried all the way home. As soon as I pulled into the driveway, I saw my dog waiting for me, tail wagging and happy to see me. I would have been lost without her as my companion. Shortly after I came back home, my daughter and her husband came by to get something out of the garage. The brief bit of friendly, human company did me good. I decided to get some fresh air to lift my spirits, so I took my dog for a walk. She loved to walk and smell her neighborhood, and doing this for her made me feel needed. I started out on my usual path, past my daughter's house, and I was not prepared for what I saw. My son and his girlfriend were at my daughter's home with her family, and William was also there. The family—*my family*—was having a Saturday get-together and I had been left out. This was my first glimpse of what I feared would become a common experience. I had my dog, and he was clinging to the kids. How could they be so thoughtless? He wanted to keep his friend and leave me hanging until he was through stroking his ego and became bored with her. He was alone because of his own greed, lust, and egocentric ways. I was the causality. I turned and walked in the opposite direction and fought back the tears for several blocks, my thoughts focused on my surroundings and my ever-loving companion, my dog. I got back home, exhausted, and settled in for a clean, clear, tension-free evening. After several weeks of sleeping in other beds, I was eager to get a good night's sleep in my own bed of the last ten or so years. I had a terrible time sleeping, though, because the bed was so uncomfortable. Sleeping alone was not the problem, because I had done this for some time now. I was confused, but decided that this too would pass, and I would adjust and be okay. I lived in the house for a month or so, but William kept coming by, usually late at night.

He would turn on the TV really loud and just sit there. He was trying to annoy me, and it was working. I contacted the police only to learn that, as long as his name was still on the mortgage and he didn't hurt me, or until I put a restraining order on him, they could not do anything. So I moved out, leaving the home I had just remodeled and the built-in swimming pool I loved and the town I had called home for thirty years. I lived with my son and his girlfriend for a short while, and then decided to stay at my mother's house. She had been a divorcee for many years and could offer advice on how to regroup. I also wanted to take advantage of getting to know her as an adult woman. It was good for both of us. The only downside was that I could not take my dog with me. I really missed my companion, but my daughter was taking good care of her for me. I got back into the job market after three or so years of absence, but this time I decided not to go back to the stressful occupation of clinical management.

Love life and it will love you back.

—*Unknown*

Chapter Three

ROCK BOTTOM

This was not something that happens to someone like me. This is what I should have thought when I woke up. But I was confused because I did not know who I was, where I was, why I was there, what had happened to me, or who all of these people were who said they knew me and loved me. I had all of these questions, but I was unable to speak. I couldn't move either. It turned out that I had suffered a brain aneurysm that had led to a stroke. I had experienced a constant headache for three days prior to this, but I had been sure it was just stress. I was sitting at my desk at work when I began hearing ripping and popping sounds in my head, and I felt as though my head was going to explode. When my ears began to ring, I knew something was terribly wrong. I walked out of my office with my purse, looked at the receptionist, and walked out of the front door. I was grateful that she followed me, and as I sat in her car, I told her that I needed to be taken to an emergency room right away. We sped off, but she was so upset and nervous that she did not know where to go. I managed to tell her to get on the freeway; there was a hospital a few exits down. I gave her my cell phone and asked her to call my mother and my girlfriend, whom I was supposed to be spending the weekend with. As we pulled up to the hospital, I began to lose consciousness. I fought it as hard as I could, but the last thing I remember was a nurse opening the car door, and the receptionist yelling for someone to help me. For the next several months, I would briefly open my eyes, my head would really hurt, and I would feel enormous pain for a few minutes before I would be put back into a medically induced coma. The hospital staff had shaved the part of my head that the doctors operated on, so I was a bit lopsided. By the time I had my third surgery, my mother asked a hairdresser to straighten up the way I looked. I guess she figured that, if I were to wake up and see myself, I would be upset. If she had known that I would have no recollection of what I was supposed to look like, then maybe she would not have worried. Being bedridden is like leaving a welcome mat out for pneumonia. I fought that battle several times. Diarrhea plagued my internal system. At times, this would be so bad that my mother would put nothing more on me than a T-shirt, split up the back to the collar so it went over my head easily, and a diaper. This made it easier to change me and clean me up. I was fortunate to not have any skin breakdowns, but that thanks is reserved for my mother for being such a cautious caregiver.

> *Only through experience of trial and suffering*
> *can the soul be strengthened, vision cleared,*
> *ambition inspired, and success achieved.*

> *—Helen Keller*

The following is a letter to me from my daughter:

> *The day of the aneurysm, I remember being called to the hospital and told to get there as soon as I could. When I arrived, I was met by Erik, along with Dave, your boss. Erik and I were taken back to see you, and you were hooked up to breathing*

machine as well as every other machine imaginable. You were unconscious. We were then taken back to speak to the doctor, but there was a discrepancy, because you and Dad were going through a divorce, so we had to get him to sign a release to allow us to make the necessary medical decisions for you. Erik and I were taken to a room, and we were given the projected outcome of your situation. We were told you had an aneurysm and that when the clot blew it was as if a small bomb had gone off in your head and caused some surrounding damage. There was no other option other than to clamp it off. I can't remember why, but they said they could not do a stent. The doctor drew a picture to show us how a stent worked and explained it, but I still don't remember the exact reason they could not do this. Other than clamping this, we could simply let you go peacefully. We asked what your chances were for surviving the surgery, and they told us 7 percent. At the time, we had pretty much decided you were already gone, but we went back to the family members who were there and told them what we had been told. There were a lot of opinions as to what we should do. The majority wanted us to try with the clamping surgery. I remember Erik saying we should probably let you go, because we didn't know what kind of damage had been done, but this did not go over well with the rest of the family. Erik and I went off to talk about it and decided, since you were more than likely not to survive the surgery, we should try, knowing we had done all that we could.

The hospital sent in a priest, and he performed your "last rights," and we all prayed. Everyone got to be alone with you for a few moments before they took you to surgery to say their good-byes. I will say that I don't think I have ever seen Erik so undone in my entire life. He just cried. When I had my time with you, I held your hand and apologized for not being able to do more. I was also selfish and asked you not to leave me yet. I remember telling you that I did not know what my kids and I were going to do without you and asking you to please fight. In my mind, I kept playing over the events of two days before, when you had come to spend the day with the kids me at our house, and I kept thinking that I should have hugged you when you left.

Anyway, they took you to surgery, and it felt like an eternity before they came out and said it had gone well, and everything looked okay. We were all shocked that you had made it through, and we could hear the operating staff celebrating.

That night, everyone but Granny and I went home. Granny and I stayed and waited to see if there would be any changes. We were not allowed to see you until the next day. From that time on, we were allowed in two at a time during visiting hours. You were kept in ICU in a medically induced coma. For days there was no real news. You had a lot of visitors. It seemed like a never-ending stream of people going in and out of your room. I remember the head nurse made a comment about you having the most visitors they had ever seen, and that you must have been an incredible person to have so many people coming to see you.

Then they allowed you to come out of the coma, and we were allowed to see you. When you opened your eyes, you just stared around with a very lost look. Nobody was certain that you knew what was going on, who we were, or that you even understood us. I believe that lasted for about a week. At that point, you started showing signs of recognition. However, it seemed as if you forgot who we were from time to time. We had to go in to reintroduce ourselves and wait to see if you seemed to notice us. You had a breathing tube down your throat so you could not respond even if you had wanted to. You appeared to have no movement on one side of your body.

From that point on, it was day to day. They finally decided to take out the breathing tube and put in a tracheal tube, because you were still not breathing well on your own, and they had to sedate you due to pain and all of the surgeries you were having. When they decided to do the tracheotomy, I believe, is also when they decided to put in your first feeding tube. At that time, Erik and I were called back in to receive an update on the new outlook to your situation. The doctor told us that you seemed to be paralyzed on the right side of your body and that they were still not sure if you really knew what was going on. They explained that the brain takes a long time to heal, and they would have no idea how much was affected until such time as you could communicate with us better. We were told that you seemed to be in the clear, but with the brain there is always a chance that you could take a turn for the worse.

You were kept in ICU after your tracheotomy and feeding tube. After a while, it was decided that you would be moved to another facility. When you got there, you were again taken directly to ICU, and Erik and I were once again given the same outlook. At that time, they asked us if we wanted to sign a DNR [do not resuscitate] since your state of health could change at any minute. They explained to us that, if you should have another stroke or any other major issue, the outcome could be catastrophic. We bounced it around a while, and then ultimately decided to sign it, because to make you suffer any *further damage seemed cruel. I remember that I decided to actually go home that night, and I just cried. I felt as if I had signed the papers to "put you to sleep." Thank God that I had my husband and Dad to talk to, and they explained to me that I was doing the right thing, because I felt horrible.*

I went back the next day, and your situation was still the same. You would open your eyes occasionally, but you didn't seem to know who we were. After a few days there, your mental state seemed to improve. We were then able to talk to you, and you seemed to understand. We decided to have you communicate with us through blinking. Once was for yes and twice was for no. That worked about 50 percent of the time, so we weren't sure how much you were really "getting."

The pulmonologist came by and told us to talk to you more. The more stimulation we could give you, the better, but we should give you breaks from time to time. That is when I decided to start reading to you. I brought a bunch of my books from home, and I would read to you for forty-five minutes to an hour at a time. Sometimes you would fall asleep and other times you would start to blink like you wanted me to stop. Also, I noticed that, if I asked you if you wanted me to stop reading, you would respond to me. During that time when I was reading and stimulating your brain, you seemed to improve in your ability to respond to us.

While I was at one particular nursing home, waiting on a bed at a rehabilitation facility, I still had a catheter, and I still had no ability to walk. I was dropped or let fall twice. Both of these times, my feeding tube became dislodged and had to be replaced. The doctors at this facility actually sewed the tube to my stomach thinking that would keep it from falling out again. They did so without numbing my skin first, and it was extremely painful. I cried and begged them not to do this, but the doctor insisted that, either way, he had to puncture my stomach, and once was enough for him. So it was to be, and from that time on, I had a fear of falling and losing my tube. This was probably the worst period for me, because my brain was healing, and I was alert enough to know where I was. I could easily see that I was one of the youngest at this facility. The "residents" were mostly older and just sat in their wheelchairs or slept. To pass the time, I would take myself to the library and stay for long periods or lie in my bed and use a laptop that had been brought to me. I watched movies and was grateful I had family members who would bring them for me to watch. The rooms were small with two twin beds each and little to no privacy. I can see why these types of facilities are depressing, and I hope and pray that I never have to go back to one.

If you don't feel it, you can't heal it.

—Unknown

As I said, this was a sad place to be. I was ultimately in five different facilities for twelve whole months. I do not remember the first three, and can remember only some of the fourth and all of the fifth. I absolutely loved TIRR Memorial Hermann, a rehabilitation facility in Houston, Texas. I know my kids tried hard to get me accepted, and I am so thankful that they did. I learned so much, and to this day, I still quote many of the therapists. I still practice the lessons I learned there, and I will continue to do so for as long as I am able. The real lessons began after I finally got to go home and began my new and very different way of life. A good friend once told me that my recovery did not begin until I returned home after the hospital.

I cried when she said this, but she was absolutely right. I am still learning something new each and every day, and that is a good thing. Who do you know who does not have a health issue to learn to live with? My bet is, if you think about it, you will find that many disabilities or challenges affect people of every shape, age, color, and size. The option to stop learning is not a good one for me, because it would mean I have stopped living. I have a feeding tube, balance issues, I am blind in my right eye, have paralysis on the right side of my throat, speak very softly, and have many scars in very visible places. With all of this, I still feel this world has a lot to offer, and I believe that I have a lot to offer to it yet too.

Choose to be happy each day.

—*Unknown*

Chapter Four

ON MY WAY BACK UP

While I don't remember much about the lost year, I can offer some insights. The thing to remember is that the medical professionals are somewhat numb to what patients are going through. By this, I mean they do not realize that patients are probably not as familiar with the *why.* My request to them would be that they fill their patients in with regard to the what and why instead of simply ordering them to do something. I found it was helpful, as well as motivating, if my caregivers explained the possible results of a practice or procedure to me up front and did not rely on me to ask questions. I was very overwhelmed with all that was going on, and I am sure it seemed oftentimes to my medical professionals that I was not concerned or not "connected." Dealing with an aneurysm was new to me as well as to my family members, so to us, the roadway to recovery was unchartered territory. There were times when I would hallucinate and seem to be alert, but I remember little to none of it now. My family would simply go along with me and laugh to each other, but allowed me to express my "thoughts." This was helpful to my recovery and to my memory. The flashbacks I still have are foggy, so I am not sure if they are real or something I just imagined. There will always be questions for me and for my family members, and my friends know that, while they might think of all the past events as old, they are new to me. If you find yourself in my predicament or know someone who has had a similar injury, you can benefit from my experience. Please allow these people to express themselves and to ask as many questions they need to in order to feel comfortable and get the closure they need. Moving forward can be frustrating, and is hard enough without the extra burden of anger or the haunting unease of unanswered questions. Another end result of being an in-house patient for a year is that my sleeping schedule has been reprogrammed. I am now unable to sleep more than four hours at a time without waking up. There were always noises, smells, or someone coming into the room to do a job at all hours of the day and night. The worst for me personally were the constant beeping noises. To this day I cannot stand to hear that particular sound. With different physical limitations and a feeding tube, sleep positions are minimal. I can sleep only in an elevated position, on my back or right side. I was told that, for most of us, our bodies adjust for our slumber, and saliva production is significantly less during our sleeping moments. What little we do have automatically goes down our throats. Mine goes straight to my lungs, because my throat is paralyzed on one side. I am usually able to expel most of it when I awake, which is good because it will cause pneumonia, which I have had several times. The medical professionals were constantly changing my medications. I now know (and remember from my medical background) that it is a trial-and-error game. I know that certain elements of medicines are backed by research and science, but we are all individuals and respond differently. The addition of medication by each specialized professional who treats a patient seems to be common. It is left up to the patients, with the help of their primary care doctors, to decide if they want to continue all of the drugs once they get home. I am not talking about the medications for your physical health, but the medications for mental health should be looked at closely. I was sent home with a prescription that said to take four doses a day of a potent psychotropic medication, a type of medication that affects the mind, emotions, and behavior. I know that the doctors were attempting to "help" me by calming me, but these drugs are very habit forming. I learned that the hard way. I had to endure withdrawal symptoms of sweats and mood swings in order to get myself straightened out. It is, of course, a personal choice for each one of us, but I believe that the fewer foreign substances you can put in your body, the better. A common side effect of a stroke, and of certain drugs, is an unsteady gait or loss of balance. I still fall, cannot multitask, and I am slower than I used to be. Some of these symptoms have actually improved, but even what remains is not accepted as "normal" by society. There is something to be said for stopping to smell the roses. This life is special, and each moment should be celebrated and acknowledged. I wish I had realized this a long time ago.

I would like to share some of the lessons that I learned about eating with a feeding tube. I have had to learn how to deal with having a feeding tube and how much everything we do or say is almost always food oriented. There are holidays, birthdays, anniversaries, showers, weddings, reunions … and the list goes on and on. Most people take eating and drinking at will for granted—until they can no longer do those things on their own. There are some who will be uncomfortable, and they can't help the way they feel any more than they can help that the fact that the feeding tube is the way they must sustain their lives. Don't take it personally. Eating can be a challenge when you live with a feeding tube. If people are like me, they may not want to be hooked up continuously to a machine like they were in the hospital for meals, or even hooked up only at night. Bolus feeding was the only answer left for me. In this method liquid food is introduced, usually three times a day, directly into the stomach or intestines through a tube. It offers so much more flexibility than continuous feeding.

I found that the clothing I wore made a difference as to where and how I could "eat." A dress was impossible, because in order to access the tube, which is in the abdomen, you'd have to raise the dress over your hips. This can be done only if you are in a bathroom or another small, private room. The way to go is a two-piece outfit. I wear dresses only to special occasions or to church—any outing that is going to last no longer than three or four hours.

Here are my suggestions: When you want to go somewhere, you have to plan your trip around your feeding schedule, kind of the way you would if you were traveling with a baby. I call my "feeding bag" my "diaper bag." If you are going out, you have to be sure you have food blended before you leave. You also will need water, syringe (used to inject the food into the tube), medication, medication crusher, napkins, hand sanitizer, and tubing for the minimum amount of time you will be away from home. I usually include enough food and water for unplanned time away; if you are running late or if you have a problem, for example. You can't just grab a bite to eat or a drink at a drive-thru on your way home.

Getting used to "eating" in public is a little tricky. Some people will look at you with disgust, and some with curiosity. I have even seen small children start to cry because they were scared. The trick is acting as if it is normal (and it is your new normal) and making sure those with you act as if it is normal as well.

And then, there is the food. It's everywhere. You can't watch TV, read a magazine, listen to the radio, or drive anyplace without seeing or smelling food. If you go to the movie theatre, you're going to smell the popcorn before you walk through the doors, and then you'll see all the different candies and fast foods. If you go to a shopping mall, there is always a food court. Don't even get me started on going to the grocery store. Every holiday, weekend, special occasion, or event is centered on food.

What is a girl supposed to do about dating? Meeting for a drink of any kind or going out to eat is not an option anymore. Well, okay, you can still go, but your date has to eat or drink alone. It takes a lot of courage, acceptance, and humor to survive not being able to swallow. Most people, including myself at one time in my life, take tasting and smelling all of the different cuisines for granted. It is hard not to feel like a freak.

Multitasking is no longer an option if you are eating or drinking, because it takes both hands and your complete attention. I can honestly say I won't be stopped for drinking and driving because I can't! The one thing some tube feeders are able to do is taste. This is because a side effect of having a feeding tube is reflux. Reflux is what allows me to taste, and I am very grateful for that. This one thing has really helped me to not feel so cheated. I tried putting some food in my mouth, chewing, and then spitting it out so I could have the taste experience, but that was not for me. It seemed rude and dirty, and it is difficult to fight the natural reaction to swallow. It takes a lot of self-control not to swallow, and it just looks nasty when you spit. Reflux actually enables me to taste what goes into the feeding tube. When I realized that I could taste, it was on!

I have been through several blenders, and I have learned to keep one as a spare, just in case. I experiment with different tastes and options by blending my medical "food" with whatever I desire. Be careful, though, and watch out for things that can clog your tube, just as people who have food allergies must be vigilant not to ingest what they are allergic to.

I have included a food guide to get you started, and I hope you will be creative yourself. I have also learned to blend my meals for two to three days all at one time so I am not constantly washing the blender. Besides, it is much easier to be spontaneous when you already have food prepared.

Then you have all of the holes in your abdomen from the tubes—I am up to five now! I like to say that they are my belly buttons and they are all "innies"! I plan to pierce them someday, just for kicks or maybe take up belly dancing! To look as normal as one can, wearing-tight fitting shirts and snug pants is out of the question. High heels are out, too, if you have balance issues. When you are re-learning how to walk, fashion is no longer an option! Sometimes I would tuck my shirt in to look more put together. Then, once, I walked around in two department stores before I noticed that my shorts were unzipped. Thank goodness I had been pushing a shopping basket to help me balance and walk better. The basket, hopefully, hid the open gate! Oh well, I don't know those people, and they don't know me, so no harm was done.

So once you quit fighting the tube feeding idea, all you have to do is get used to being around food, smelling food, reading about food, hearing about food, and dressing.

The best parts—and, yes, there are good parts—are that you never have to wonder what to choose to eat, and you never have to worry much about gaining weight and dieting again. As a side note, I have told several people that I have the perfect, fail-proof diet, but no one has taken me up on choosing this way yet. I kind of like being skinny!

The subject about swimming will most likely come up, and let me just say that you can't. The hole(s) in your stomach are the perfect avenue for body fluids to get out, and the perfect opening for pollutants to get in. You can shower, but you should not sit in a body of water. You can put your feet and legs in a pool if you are strong enough to do this safely. You can lie on the water on a float if you can carefully wrap your tube, hose, and stoma (the opening in the abdomen) with plastic wrap and tape it closed so no water can penetrate it. Just don't fall into the water! Moving you arms and legs might be a problem for you as you try to keep your head above the water until help arrives.

I have also had to endure a rash from stomach fluid that can happen when the feeding tube leaks. My last placement is on the left, just below the rib cage. Each time I move, it does too. I had what was referred to as "an angry rash" by medical personnel for almost an entire year. I was referred to several types of specialists. I finally was sent to a wound care doctor whose assistant explained what was happening and showed me how to place gauze around the stoma so the tube would be snug and not leak. It took only a year of this before the gastroenterologist decided to put a different kind of feeding tube in. The one I have now is in the same hole (yay!) and was designed for more active people. It is called a "button tube," and I love it. It gives me freedom because I don't have to hide the bulky stoma and the tubing. I have a cabinet full of the different types of creams, lotions, and powders that I have tried. Oh, the joys of tube feeding!

Now, we haven't covered sex yet. Can you be sexy with a feeding tube? Right—don't go there. I cannot discuss dating either. I have been told to write only about what I know!

Be grateful for all that you have and do.

—Unknown

Chapter Five
OTHER OBSTACLES

Your smile is contagious; share it.

—Unknown

I have a paralyzed esophagus from the stroke and aneurysm, so my voice is very soft and raspy. This is the reason I had to stop going through drive-thru banks and pharmacies and other similar facilities. I became weary of having to send them my driver's license to show them who I was and then wait for them to track down why I was there. It can be difficult to be heard when there is a lot of outside noise—traffic, diesel engines, and radios. I often had the person with me do the talking from the passenger side, even when that other person was a child.

The telephone is another challenge for someone like me with dysphasia (language difficulties caused by brain disease or damage). Voice-activated services do not pick up a soft, raspy voice. I have been cursed at, hung up on, accused of being drunk, called a child, fussed at for playing on the phone, and very often, apologized to because the caller thinks he or she has just woken me up. As I said earlier, our society is not very empathetic. I experienced an episode that truly challenged my inability to be vocally loud when the door in our chicken yard got stuck and I got trapped inside. Sandy was on the outside, barking and whining because she couldn't get in. The door finally opened enough for me to squeeze through, but I was so terrified that I was in tears. I simply I couldn't yell out for help. My stepmother told me that I probably was not ready to join a particular dating site for agricultural individuals just yet. This thought got me to laugh, and my ordeal has become a family joke. I had pushed and pulled on the door so much in my state of panic that it fell off of the hinges later that same day and had to be repaired.

A speech therapist once suggested to me that I carry typed notes that explain that I have a paralyzed throat and cannot speak loudly, but I have not tried this approach. My hands are already full with the small cup I must carry at all times. I am still trying different approaches to this particular problem, and look at it as a challenge instead of a disability. I am finding that raising my hand, the way I did back in school, works well if I am in a small group and need or want to be heard. I avoid large, crowded places simply because the noise keeps me from being heard. And I tire easily over just being present and not speaking. Then there are the eating and drinking issues, so there are many obstacles to encounter. I have a confession to make: I turned fifty wearing a diaper, or pull-up, as my mother would say. I had a catheter for almost an entire year, so I went home with minimal bladder and bowel control. A urologist told me that my brain was sending mixed signals to my bladder and bowel, so my body does not always respond. To make matters worse, I continually fought diarrhea. My younger sister and I went shopping on one occasion, and I wanted to look at hats and scarves, since my head had been shaved several times. While we were in one particular accessory store, I felt a warm, mushy something running down my leg to the floor. I looked down to see that I was standing in a pool of feces. It was so runny that it had run out of the pull-up. At the time, I had a walker to get around with, so I motioned to my sister, who swept me out a side door and ran to get the car. I stood there waiting for her with my back to the brick wall so no one would see my wet, soiled rear end. We drove off quickly and didn't speak for ten minutes or so, and then she burst out laughing. She was thinking about the poor soul who had to clean up the mess. She laughed even harder when she remembered two young boys we'd seen running around the store. She said she could see one of them slipping and falling in the mess. All I could think about was that the security cameras caught what had happened and they knew how to find me—or they put it on the local news. I call that my "shitty shopping experience" now, and it has become a family joke. To this day, when we want to go shopping, we will mention the experience and laugh. Another time, I got up during the night to go to the bathroom and did not want to wake up, so I did not turn on the light. I did fine sitting down, but when I started to get up, I lost my balance and fell backward. I slipped off the toilet seat and got stuck between the toilet and the wall. There is a small ledge at the bottom of that wall. It's about six inches high, and I have put pretty glass bottles on it. One of them fell to the floor and broke. So, there I was, stuck, barefoot, and with my pants down. I should have panicked, because I live alone and did not know when I would be helped or found. Instead, I immediately got this image in my head that my dog was talking to the neighbor's sheep.

> *Be kind. All of us are on this journey, and we*
> *are all fighting a battle of some kind.*

> *—Unknown*

She was telling them that they didn't have it so bad, because her human falls off of the toilet! I started laughing and could not stop. After several minutes, I remembered the class I had taken at TIRR Memorial Hermann on how to get up after a fall. I did what they had taught me and finally got out of my situation, without even stepping on any glass! Another night I had a bad dream and woke feeling scared. I looked around and remembered that I was in my bed, and I was safe. I decided I needed to go to the bathroom, so I got out of bed. When I started to walk, I lost my balance and nearly fell. I stood there for a minute, then tried again, falling this time. I fell against the rolling desk. The desk rolled into the nightstand, the lamp fell, the bulb broke, and stuff was falling everywhere. The noise was terrible. I was so embarrassed because I was sure that the neighbors had heard all of this. As I was lying there, I thought, *I really need to get up and go to the restroom*. At about that time, Sandy, who was sleeping on the end of the bed right near me, let out a really loud snore. I burst into laughter, which woke her up. All I could think of was how my guard dog had slept through all of the racket! I was laughing so hard I wet myself and then really had a mess to clean up. Perhaps the saddest thing is that I find that people will take advantage of the fact that I had a brain injury. If I am confused because they have told me something two different ways, they suggest that it is my memory that is the problem. I try really hard to write everything down, pay close attention, and observe everything around me with the intention of remembering all that I can. I was told at TIRR Memorial Hermann that I should do things that will stimulate the brain and encourage cell growth, so I do this daily, even now. I stress daily over my knowledge and memory issues, so comments from those who have not walked a mile in my shoes truly hurt me. Of all of the funny things, I must say that the strangest for me is that I hear music in my head all of the time, even now. Apparently, while I was having the brain surgeries, the surgeon played classical music in the operating room to soothe him and help him concentrate. My brain absorbed and remembers this music even though I was not conscious at the time. At first, I was not sure if it was "angels from the choir in heaven" or if I was just a little crazy! The elderly gentleman my mother cares for actually believes that I am mentally challenged! He will speak to me, but he directs his questions or remarks to someone else as though I cannot understand him.

A day without laughter is a day wasted.

—Charlie Chaplin

I will occasionally mess with him, just to be sure I can still laugh. After a few years, I went back to visit the first facility in which I had been hospitalized. I wanted to meet some of the professionals who had cared for me, say thank you, and see where I had started my journey. Because so much time had elapsed, some people had moved on. Some who were still there were working different shifts. But I did get to meet the surgeon who had performed the life-saving surgery and tell him that I was eternally grateful to him. I thanked him for allowing God to work through his hands. He simply smiled and said that he was happy to have been a part of my journey. Staff members in the ICU where I spent several months unconscious told me that it was rare for them to see how patients were doing after they left their facility. I hope that others understand the importance of gratitude and recognition, and go back to hospitals where they have been cared for to and say how they appreciate the care they received. That simple act can "make the day" for medical professionals and encourage them to continue caring for the ill and injured. While my family members watched over me, they decided to keep a journal in my room. Visitors recorded their names, the date and time of their visit, and any information that was relevant at the time. That way, everyone who came in could find out what had been going on at any given time. This was a great way to communicate, and it also was a way to preserve stories of the now-funny things that occurred as well as some not-so-funny moments. This journal was misplaced during one of my moves, so the contents were lost. I can now reference my past experiences only through my murky memories. Being blind in my right eye has been particularly hard for me. I had to have it sewed surgically to a semi-shut position to protect it from getting an infection. My face is numb on the right side, so I don't feel much of anything until pain really sets in. Vision is another area that seems to be taken for advantage by most. I have found that seeing well with one eye not only gives me a headache, but it creates a glare on bright objects. My patience is tested regularly because I do not see clearly. I frequently drop things, because I do not judge distance correctly. I have learned to drive adjusting for the vision issues, but I drive only locally or to places that I can get to along a familiar route. I depend on others to help with the longer trips. At least I can drive enough so I do not feel stuck in one place; I can still be independent. What I have to continually say to myself is that I have come so far from where I was, I have learned a great deal, and I have met some really good people. Every day I can get out of bed on my own, and no matter how hard it may be, it is still a good day. I look forward, not backward, and I pray that you do too. Here are some ways that family members and friends can help you to make the transition:

They can remind you to:

- Maintain personal hygiene (brush your teeth, wash your hair, bathe, shave, and so forth)
- Wear appropriate undergarments (sometimes you may need reminding!)
- Dress, fix hair, do your makeup daily—even if you don't plan to leave the house
- Stay busy—it helps you not to focus on feeling any pain
- Stay connected to friends and family

Tell your family and friends:

- Don't be afraid to say no.
- Don't be afraid to speak the truth.
- It is okay to say things that are not normal, and that goes for both of you.
- TV, radio, cards, games—all of these things are okay, just don't force them on you.

You need to remember:

- They are willing to "do" for you; don't feel guilty—they love you.
- They are willing to give their time and company. Sometimes that can cost you a whole lot more in extra pain and humility as well as loss of time and money.
- Say please and thank you to everyone, and say I love you. Tomorrow may never come.
- Sometimes a person just needs to cry; it relieves the locked-up emotions.
- You have to get used to thinking and doing for yourself again.

- You have to get used to carrying money in a purse or wallet again.
- Treat others who are around you with respect; it is not their fault you are ill.
- Write your directive to physicians, a living will, and all other advance wishes and discuss them all with your family. This is not being morbid or being a martyr; it is just practical.
- Put a list in your wallet/purse of all your medications and doctors, along with their contact information.
- Create a timeline that lists procedures, surgeries, and hospitals along with diagnoses, dates, and treatments. Carry it with you to each new doctor.
- Choose to be happy each day.
- When you see someone who is in a wheelchair or on oxygen (someone who is handicapped or disabled in some way), don't just smile and pass on by; rather, take a moment to think about why they are in that condition and know that they would rather not be the way they are.
- Love life, and it will love you back.
- Keep yourself busy so you are not focused on how bad you might feel.
- Learn all that you can, because knowledge is something no one can take away from you.
- Be grateful for all that you have and do. When you are feeling unsure, just turn on the television or look around you, and you will see sadness and need.
- Your smile is contagious, so share it.
- Use your down time or healing time to inform and educate yourself. You are your own best advocate.
- Take time to rest so your body can heal, but remember that an active mind means an active body.

- Pray and go to church.
- Giving to make others feel better is the quickest way to feel better yourself!

Mind reading has not yet been perfected, so don't expect someone to "just know." I remember feeling abandoned and hurt after I got home because everyone went back to work and picked up the pieces of their lives, which they'd been neglecting. I had a hard time realizing they were not neglecting me; they were just glad things were getting back to normal.

Joy balances the fear with love.

—Unknown

I feel as though I need to share this letter that I wrote to my family so you will know that I try to walk the walk, not just talk the talk:

May 14, 2012

Change of Habits

After long consideration of my new way of life, I have come to these conclusions with regard to you, my family members.

I promise to:

- *Be more understanding of your time and thoughts*
- *Remember that you work*
- *Adjust to being around food*
- *Start cooking again for all of you*
- *Learn how to be single*

I know you have all been taking care of me for over two years, and I can only say thank you and that I am sorry. I have been married since I was seventeen years old, so I have to learn how to be single now. I was just starting to adjust when I was rendered helpless by the stroke and brain aneurysm. I went from a house, to an upstairs, to a small bedroom, and then to five different health facilities. I lost everything. After one whole year in hospitals, I became dependent on others to help me.

I know that I have said that I don't want to be around food, and I know how uncomfortable you feel eating around me, so we will all have to get used to the new normal. I can still cook—I can taste the food to know what it needs; I just can't swallow it!

I am not blaming anyone. I take responsibility for my own actions, and I am as much at fault as William with the divorce. Please bear with me, and do not be afraid to speak your mind. I will listen and be fair. I know it is not all about just me. I can't bear being left out by my own family, or at least feeling as though I am. I am also aware of how lucky I am to finally have privacy again, and this house to live in, rent free. I could not be living alone any other way.

I was used to working and want to feel as though I am part of the solution, not the problem again. I think that this emotion is the hardest. I will work harder to adjust, and I ask each of you to please do the same.

I love you all.

PS: I call dibs on the next holiday (if I have a stove to cook on)!

I am worthy of love.

—*Natalie Ledwell*

Going Home and What to Expect

- There are going to be bad days (shitty days!).
- You are going to be fussed at.
- You will be treated differently.

I was once told that a patient's real recovery did not begin until after he or she left the hospital and went home—no matter if the hospital stay lasted one day, one week, one month, or one whole year. This is not meant to discourage you. I want you and your support group to be aware of the challenges ahead. Most people believe (you may even think this too) that you are well once you are able to go home from the hospital. With a major illness, that could not be further from the truth. All going home really means is that your insurance company has most likely told your doctor or the hospital that they will not approve payment for anymore days, or that your lifetime maximum allowable has been reached. Once you get home, the real work begins. Your home might resemble a hospital in many areas, particularly the bedroom and the bathroom. You will have medical supplies; medicines; and papers full of information, instructions, and schedules. If you have visiting nurses or physical or occupational therapists, you will be expected to eat, sleep, and drink around their busy schedules. No one told me how painful therapy can be; perhaps they did not want to stress me with the information. If you were unlucky enough to have had brain damage, you will probably have a speech therapist as well as the others. Don't forget, you will have doctor appointments to keep and follow-ups with the surgeons and other specialists. Our society is one that is always rushed and in a hurry. People multitask and expect you to keep up or get out of their way. They can be less than empathic and patient. Do not take this personally. If you are in a wheelchair, people may crowd you, step in front of you, or just stare at you. If you are unable to walk quickly, you may be pushed and frowned upon for not moving fast enough. I have been fussed at for not having strength or good balance by a hurried professional. Just remember, you are special and you matter. We all heal differently, and we do not understand this until we are forced to find out through experience.

Excursions out just for a change of scenery can be difficult. The big glass doors on most buildings are extremely heavy and hard to open. To be completely honest, I thought they were heavy before my stroke and aneurysm. If you are lucky, you will have someone strong who can pack, unpack, push, and pull the wheelchair or open those heavy doors. Going to a park or somewhere where with sand and rock underfoot can be hard on you and your helper. If you are weak, it is best to go to places at times when the crowds are smaller and there are sure to be places where you can sit and rest. A building with more than one floor can be challenging too. Most buildings have elevators and handicapped entrances, but remember to think about escaping in case of a fire. If you are walking, but having some difficulties, you may want to avoid places where there are only stairs. Be sure to get a handicap parking permit if possible. This one little item will help you in a big way. I still stumble and lose my balance today, but when I do, I make sure I am okay, and my tube is still in place. I get up, dust off, and continue on. Getting upset or stressing that others have seen you does nothing for the situation. Besides, you know what I have said about crying!

My life is filled with abundance.

—*Natalie Ledwell*

Chapter Six

HELPFUL FOOD-RELATED TIPS

Helpful Tips

- Wear something that unbuttons. Wearing any two-piece outfit, you can enjoy your day out.
- Always take your syringe with you to ensure you are able to eat. (I keep a spare one in the glove box in my car or in my purse.)
- Remember to plan your outings and take appropriate steps to get your nourishment.
- Four teaspoons of Ovaltine each morning with "milk" provides all the vitamins you need (and it tastes good!).
- Others may feel nervous about you "eating" in front of them. Remember to smile and tell them politely that this is your new way. If you act as though nothing is wrong, then they will be less likely to feel nervous.
- Keep containers of your favorite foods in the freezer to enjoy, and put one in the refrigerator to thaw as you need it. (This works great for items from the grocery store or cooked items.)
- If you're going out, take a "to go" container with you so you can bring home food.

Go through your cookbooks or magazines, and don't be afraid or say "I can't." Prepare or buy the foods you have always liked, just be careful not to clog your tube. I could put all of my "favorite" recipes here, but I would have too many pages to type. My goal is to encourage you to play with your own ideas and enjoy life with your feeding tube.

I have heard "think outside of the box" all of my life, but I say "think outside of your feeding tube and thoughts"!

I radiate love and happiness every single day.

—Natalie Ledwell

I carry a separate bag with all of the necessary items I need in order to eat. I call it my diaper bag. I even have a small towel to cover my lap in case of a spill.

Diaper bag contents:

- Water, 16 or so ounces
- Hand sanitizer
- One (12-ounce) bottle of Coke (It's the secret to clear a clogged feeding tube!)
- Meal, prepared earlier, in a capped container
- Small towel
- Napkins
- Feeding syringe (and tubing)
- Any medications you may need, along with a medicine crusher
- A spare plastic cup (for spitting in, because you can't swallow)

I am successful in everything I do.

—Natalie Ledwell

Chapter Seven

A NEW WAY OF THINKING (THE NEW NORMAL)

When people experience something like a stroke or they get a devastating disease, it generally turns them into better people. I find that life has much more meaning now, and I appreciate it more. There is heartache where there was none before. I guess I feel weaker in some areas, but I feel stronger in the areas that are more important now like life, love, family, and God. Slowing down and enjoying the small, simple things has become important to me now. Religion and God have become more important too.

When you think about where you have been and where you have not been, there will more than likely be some making up to do. I have wakened each day grateful to be alive. I thank the good Lord for everything. I also remember to say please, thank you, and I love you a whole lot more. I am more able to excuse others and feel empathy for them on a deeper level. I love deeper too.

I have come to realize that all we really have are our families and friends. My priorities have been rearranged, and what was once important no longer matters. As I said, I am a better person now. I have always said that, once an event or opportunity goes by, it cannot be retrieved, but now I feel that sentiment and realize it even more. Where your experience may feel new to you, remember that it is past news to most of those who cared for you, so just be grateful that you survived.

Human beings are funny creatures. We have all these emotions and thoughts about how we think things should be. If life throws us a curve ball, we want to immediately blame someone or something. Perhaps it is time to just be grateful for all that we do have and focus on that instead of the things that we want. We all live on this planet together, so we might as well honor one another.

> *Your task is not to seek for love, but merely to seek and find all of the barriers you have built against it.*
>
> *—Unknown*

My grandmother used to say that sometimes God makes you lie down so that you can look up. I am very grateful that he did just that to me. I have met some incredible people along the way, and I have learned some valuable lessons about myself that I would not have learned had he not gotten my attention. My lying down came when I had a brain aneurism, which led to a stroke. I spent one whole year in five different facilities to recover from that. I was unconscious for the first five months, had my last rights said over me, was paralyzed on my right side, had my head shaved three different times, and had to have a feeding tube inserted in my stomach in order to get fluids and nutrition. I have a shunt in my head and two pins. I had pneumonia several times, which left me in isolation without a bed bath for days at a time. I was eventually able to walk again, after repeated painful physical therapy sessions. I had occupational therapy to teach me how to hold my head up straight, use my arms and hands, and how to write and spell again. The most important of these classes taught me how to apply makeup again! I also had an aide who showed me how to properly tie a scarf on my head so I would look good after my hair was shaved for surgery. I can tell you that I have about fifteen scarves to date, and hats as well!

It was exhausting just to be out of bed, and my head would spin. My body had to readjust to everyday experiences. Before that the aneurism and stroke, I had been diagnosed with polymyositis (a muscle disease that acts like cancer and attacks the extremities, heart, lungs, and throat) and had taken ten months of chemotherapy in pill form. On top of all that, I became single again after thirty years of marriage. I decided then that, when you change the way you look at things, things will change. I decided I was going to be a fighter.

While I was in the fifth facility, I met a chaplain who came to visit and talk to me once a week. I looked forward to her visits, and through her I was born again. I started saying the rosary each night before I went to sleep. I had always believed in God, but after my grandmother passed away, I had slipped away from my faith. The last three years or so had brought me back to the teachings I had received as a young child.

I finally was released to go home, but was only allowed to go to places where there would be constant supervision. I went to stay at my mother's home and began my long road to gaining my independence back. I don't know why, but I actually believed that I would miraculously heal once I was home. I was wrong, but I did enjoy the privacy and the quiet again. I had endured listening to machines beeping and the sound of sirens. I had endured interruptions throughout the night, lack of sleep, grueling physical therapy schedules, fear, loneliness, and depression. I had missed my dog's companionship. A friend told me that my first day of recovery actually began the day I got home. I did not want to believe her then, but she was right. The one thing I can tell you is that family members and friends are prone to believe that you are recovered as well and don't call or come to see you. You get a feeling of being abandoned or left behind. I would cry when I thought about this, because I was trying so hard to regain my independence. I live alone now with my dog, and I am grateful to all of the doctors, nurses, aides, therapists, friends, and family members who helped me get here. I thank God for allowing me to live and recover to the point that I have advanced to today. I still have a feeding tube, but I have learned how to process food in the blender. I now weigh over a hundred pounds. I believe that even, though you tube feed, you do not have to have a boring diet.

I would tell anyone and everyone to not take anything for granted. Have love, which will give you faith. Have faith, which will give you strength. Never give up, because the only one who suffers then is you. You are a child of God. God made you, and God can heal you. Let your wishes be known to your family so they are not faced with the stress of making your decisions for you. It is the only sure way to be treated the way you want to be treated. While this seems like a depressing subject, it is really one that should be looked at with love. I encourage everyone to write everything down and keep these documents in a safe place, because someday, God may make you lie down to look up.

My experiences have made me a better person. I believe I am a better mother, daughter, sister, and friend than I was before all of this. Life can be challenging, but it can be rewarding too. You have a choice everyday:

Through my journey, I started journaling to help ease the pain of all that I was going through. I wrote a book and created a line of divorce greeting cards. I drew the characters, came up with the sayings, and had a logo made for the cards. I would find myself laughing and crying at the same time. I knew in my heart that others needed to laugh at their situation too. In the book, I shared my experiences gathered from the facility notes, my family's memories, and from my own notes. The book title is how I was feeling then and now, and it is full of *dos* and *don'ts*, with plenty of laughter. The old adage that when life gives you lemons, make lemonade would certainly apply here.

Do or do not, there is no try.

—Yoda
*(Fictional character from George Lucas's **Star Wars**)*

Not So Broken
A Food Guide for Tube Feeders so We Don't Feel Cheated

I have been experiencing different ways to live and be happy with my new normal. My biggest complaint is the fact that there is so much emphasis on food in television and radio commercials, billboards, and on holidays. What is a sane person to do? I put this food guide together for you in hope that you will try my way, or better yet, discover your own way. With or without insurance to help you, there are ways to keep yourself from being bored. I have been on Fibersource medical food supplement for the last five years. I started adding food to the supplement and liquefying the "concoction" in a blender after I unsuccessfully spent six months trying to gain weight beyond ninety-eight pounds. I am happy to say that I weigh a whole 107 now! Keep in mind that each person is different, and likes and dislikes will occur. Remember, my illness is as personal to me as yours is to you … not one of us is more important than the other.

I Have a Funny Story to Share

I really wanted a beer. I had drunk wine and beer in the past and even dabbled in mixed drinks. Well, I went to the grocery store and bought a six-pack of Coronitas, came back home, and eagerly started drinking a beer. Well, I was in such a hurry that I didn't think about how fast I was drinking. I quickly learned that I essentially have a built in beer bong. Needless to say, the beer tasted much better going down than it did coming back up! If you decide to enjoy an adult beverage, do it slowly, as if you are sipping it out of the cup. Learn from my mistake.

Heat and Herbs

I have learned that foods that are too hot or too cold cramp my stomach. To help with too cold, I use the microwave. Thirty seconds is all it takes to warm food up.

I have gotten back to gardening and cooking. That alone has helped my rehabilitation, both physically and mentally (I call it dirt therapy). I can eat and taste thanks to reflux; it just happens differently from it does for everyone else.

I love to grow and dry my own herbs. They have a much stronger smell and look so much darker and prettier than the herbs you buy at the grocery store. As a bonus, you only need a small amount because they are stronger in flavor as well. Play with the herbs and create your own favorites. My personal favorites are sage, curry, and curly celery.

Vegetable gardening has become one of my favorite pastimes again. You can do this, share your canned goodies, and even give them as gifts on the holidays. Just because you don't "eat" the same way is no reason not to do the things that you enjoy.

How to Unclog Your Feeding Tube

On several occasions my feeding tube has become clogged. I tried fresh strawberries once—too many seeds, I guess. If that happens to you, first of all, don't panic. Coca Cola has been used for a very long time, and it is effective in clearing the blockage. Besides, nothing beats a good old Coke burp!

The first time my tube was clogged, I panicked and called the nurse helpline listed on my insurance card. She said, "You can go for two days without eating." I was floored, and then I realized she was trying to get me to relax. Now I laugh at this statement, and it has become a joke.

Simple "Drinks"

To break away from boredom, just add any of these to your "milk" and shake really well or put the mix in your blender. I have even tried soy milk as a base.

- Any flavored cocoa mix
- Gatorade/Powerade
- Tea
- Coffee
- Cappuccino
- Orange juice ... without the pulp
- Kool-Aid

Did you know that you can get iced coffee at McDonald's without the ice?

Sweet Tooth

Add any of these to your "milk" and put the mix in your blender.

- Cookies (without coconut or nuts) (My personal favorite is gingersnaps.)
- Pudding, any flavor (even rice pudding)
- Yogurt, any flavor, but pay special attention so you don't clog the tube
- Pie (buttermilk is my personal favorite)
- Brownies (without the nuts) (Try adding peanut butter morsels ... yum!)

- Cupcakes
- Donuts
- Ice cream, any flavor (Avoid ones with coconut and nuts.)
- Cake
- Honey buns

What I am attempting to show you is that you can try basically anything you have a taste for.

Main Course Meals

I use about one-third cup of whatever I am going to "eat," put it in the blender, microwave if too cold, and three to four tablespoons of water if it's too thick, and enjoy. Just because you have a feeding tube is no reason to stop enjoying those foods you splurged on before. Experiment; just be careful.

- Pasta
- Baked chicken
- Flavored mashed potatoes
- Grits
- Oatmeal
- Cereal (I tried Chocolate Cheerios)
- Sweet potato patties or canned, baked sweet potatoes
- Fried fish (just be careful of the bones)
- Brisket
- Hamburger helper
- Macaroni and cheese
- Chili
- PO-boys (without lettuce)
- Hamburgers (without cheese or lettuce)
- Fried chicken (just be careful of the gristle and bones)

- Scrambled eggs seasoned with herbs
- Chicken and turkey pot pies
- Chicken and dumplings
- Rice, seasoned any way you like it

I have personally tried and liked the foods in this list. I have also tried pizza, but it clogged my feeding tube. Again, I add about one-third cup of the food along with a small amount of water if the mixture is too thick.

I try to keep a back-up blender just in case I wear one out! There is nothing more disheartening than turning on your blender only to find it doesn't work. This has happened to me a couple of times. At first I panicked, but then I just improvised and used my food processor until I had time to go and purchase a new blender.

If you are in the mood for a certain food at a fast food restaurant, buy it and take it home to put in the blender.

Other Interesting Add-Ins

- Peanut butter
- Molasses
- Honey
- Salad dressing
- Flavored coffee creamers
- Flavored drink syrups
- Ice cream toppers (liquid only)

Walk through the grocery store and take the time to explore all of your options. I was initially reluctant to go to the grocery store, but now I enjoy shopping.

My Personal Favorite "Recipes"

Chocolate Sugar: Combine 1 cup of sugar and ¼ cup of cocoa in a jar. Add a vanilla bean and shake to mix. After a week or two, the vanilla flavor will be absorbed by the sugar.

Chocolate Drink: Combine one cup of almond-flavored soy milk with ¼ cup of chocolate sugar (recipe above) and shake well.

Summer Veggies: Make one cup cooked pasta, any shape. Put a tablespoon of margarine in a skillet. Add two small tomatoes, cut up; yellow squash, cut into small pieces; ¼ teaspoon minced garlic; salt and pepper to taste. I also like to add 1 teaspoon tarragon. This can be done with any veggies you may have or really like.

Energy Drink: Mix in your blender one cup of cranberry juice and seven to eight fresh, home- grown baby spinach leaves.

Chicken and Mashed Potatoes: Add about 1/3 cup of baked chicken or rotisserie chicken to about 1/3 cup of mashed potatoes. You can even add gravy. Put it all in a blender, and you can experience tasting an awesome meal.

Rice with Fresh Dill: Make one serving of basmati rice. Add about two tablespoons of margarine, salt to taste, and ¼ cup fresh, clean, chopped dill.

Turkey with Cranberries: Add about ¼ cup cooked turkey and about 1/3 cup jelled cranberry sauce to a container of formula or milk and blend.

Seasoned Crackers: Add six to eight seasoned crackers (recipe to follow) to one container of formula or 1 cup soy milk. Blend in blender. (To make the seasoned crackers: Combine the following ingredients in a large bowl: 1 box of crackers; 1 package salad dressing mix such as parmesan, garlic, or ranch; 1 cup canola oil; 1/3 cup olive oil; 2 teaspoons crushed dried curly celery; and 2 teaspoons crushed red pepper. Cover for twenty-four hours, turning at least three or four times. I use these in place of chips or as a topping for a casserole dish.)

I hope that, by experimenting with what tastes you like and the variety available of foods, you will be eager to have some fun. Focus on the fact that you may be tube feeding, but all of your "needs" are essentially met. You are a child of God, and you are perfect just the way you are. Remember above all to have fun, keep your sense of humor, and be grateful that you are alive.

Note: I had a low-profile tube inserted in October of 2014. I love the freedom I experience, because it is less bulky to hide; however, it clogs easily. If you have one of these tubes, I recommend that you thin your feeding with water until you become more familiar with your specific tube.

So you're a little different— I like to think of it as special!

With God all things are possible. That's the Law of Grace.

—Dr. Susan Shumsky

Blurb for *I Am Not Broken*

Achievements made by this author in recognition for her for her contributions, determination, and insight:

- She was awarded an Eppy in 2014 for contributing to a book co-authored by multiple authors
- She was featured in Published magazine in 2014
- She had an article published in Leader magazine in 2014
- Was voted Woman of the Year for 2012/2013
- Had 4 of her personal designs in a retail magazine in 2008

Jo M is an active and contributing member of her local church and believes that if Jesus can forgive, then so can we. Love, learning, teaching and shining her light is her new way of life.

This story is not unique, it is inspirational and offers strategies to get you or your loved one on the road to recovery.

Printed in the United States
By Bookmasters